RENEGADE

C000132051

Soho Theatre and Renegade present

shraddhā

by Natasha Langridge

First performed at Soho Theatre on 29 October 2009

Soho Theatre is supported by ACE, Bloomberg,
TEQUILA\London, Westminster City Council,
The City Bridge Trust

Performances in the Lorenz Auditorium
Registered Charity No: 267234

Soho Theatre and Renegade present

shraddhā

by Natasha Langridge

Cast

Pearl **Jade Williams**

Joe **Alex Waldmann**

Ann **Miranda Foster**

Granny **Anna Carteret**

Dean **Jim Pope**

Musician **Aidan Broadbridge**

Writer **Natasha Langridge**

Director **Lisa Goldman**

Designer **Jon Bausor**

Lighting Designer **Philip Gladwell**

Sound Designer **Matt McKenzie**

Production Manager **Matt Noddings**

Stage Manager **Marie Costa**

Deputy Stage Manager **Anna-Maria Casson**

Assistant Director **Damian Le Bas**

Fight Director **Bret Yount**

Dialect Coach **Jan Haydn Rowles**

Assistant Stage Managers **Lauren Harvey & Ben Ainsley**

Assistant Designer **Matt Hellyer**

Wardrobe Supervisor **Sydney Florence**

Movement Director **Ann Yee**

Prop Maker **Becky May**

Casting Director **Nadine Rennie**

Thanks to BasketBasket, DairyCrest, Orchard Home and Gifts, Electrolux, Waterford Crystal, Theatre Royal Stratford East.

ANNA CARTERET GRANNY

Theatre includes: **Burnt by the Sun**, **Never So Good**, **Single Spies**, **Sisterly Feelings**, **Man and Superman**, **Saturday Sunday Monday**, **John Gabriel Borkman**, **Cyrano**, **The Merchant of Venice**, **Tis Pity She's a Whore**, **The National Health**, **Jumpers**, **The Advertisement**, **Danton's Death** (National Theatre); **Tom & Viv** (Almeida Theatre); **Nathan the Wise**, **Daughters of Men** (Hampstead Theatre); **Sitting Pretty** (Watford Palace Theatre); **Dona Rosita** (Orange Tree Theatre); **Absolutely Perhaps** (Wyndhams Theatre); **Copenhagen** (Michael Codron & Lee Dean Productions); **Naked Justice** (West Yorkshire Playhouse and Tour); **Heartbreak House**, **Semi Detached** (Chichester Festival Theatre); **Death of a Salesman** (Birmingham REP); **Richard III** (RSC tour and West End); **Major Barbara**, **Misanthrope** (Piccadilly Theatre); **Waste**, **King Lear** (Old Vic); **An Ideal Husband** (Haymarket and New York); **On Approval** (Playhouse Theatre); **Les Liaisons Dangereuses** (RSC Tour); **A Doll's House** (Riverside Theatre); **A Piece of My Mind** (Apollo Theatre); **The Beaux' Stratagem** (Lyric Hammersmith). Television includes: **Poirot**, **Holby City**, **Peak Practice**, **Eskimo Day/Cold Enough for Snow**, **Sherlock Holmes**, **Ashenden**, **The Shell Seekers**, **In the Heat of the Day**, **Being Normal**, **Juliet Bravo**, **The Pallisers**, **Fathers and Families** and **Glittering Prizes**. Radio includes: **Major Barbara**, **A Fairly Honorable Defeat**, **Filet de Sole Véronique**, **Literary Walks** and **A Man's Job Alone**.

MIRANDA FOSTER ANN

Miranda trained at Webber Douglas.
Theatre includes: **Romeo and Juliet** (Shakespeare's Globe); **Greenwash** (Orange Tree Theatre); **Born in the Gardens** (Rose Theatre and Bath Theatre Royal); **Shadow Language** (Theatre 503); **Festen** (UK Tour);

The Memory of Water (Watford Palace Theatre); **King Cromwell, Summer Again, The Marrying of Ann Leete** (Orange Theatre); **The Lucky Ones** (Hampstead Theatre); **Love You Too** (The Bush Theatre); **Pera Palas** (The Gate/NT Studio); **The Criminals** (Lyric, Hammersmith); **The People Downstairs** (Young Vic); **Noises Off** (UK Tour); **Hamlet, As You Like It** (Acter USA Tour); **Blithe Spirit** (Royal Exchange); **Our Country's Good, A Doll's House** (Leicester Haymarket); **The Cherry Orchard** (Aldwych Theatre).

Extensive work for the National Theatre includes: **Gilgamesh, Schism in England, King Lear, Anthony and Cleopatra, Neaptide, The Women, The Futurists, Pravda, The Government Inspector, Animal Farm, Strider, The Story of a Horse, The Spanish Tragedy, The Fawn.**

Television includes: **The Trial of Gemma Lang, Rosemary & Thyme, The Bill, Doctors, Dream Team, Where the Heart Is, Holby City, Brotherly Love, The Knock, Casualty, Sharman, The Turnaround Thin Ice, David Storey's The Contractor, Cockles** and **The Merry Wives of Windsor** (BBC Shakespeare Series).

Short film includes: **Beggar's Belief.**

JIM POPE DEAN

Theatre includes: **Car** and **Cool Water Murder** (Theatre Absolute); **The Cherry Orchard, Buried Alive, The Black Dahlia, Demons and Dybbuks** (Mike Alfred's Method and Madness); **Edward II** (Fallen Angel Theatre Co); **Man Beast and Virtue** (Great Eastern Stage tour); **Flight** (New Perspectives Theatre Company); **Iago** (The Steam Factory). He was a founder member of The Work Theatre Collective and performed in **Project B** (directed by Matthew Dunster), **Project C** (directed by Drew Pautz) and **Project E** (directed by Drew Pautz). Television includes: **The Bill, Doctors, Casualty, Planet Earth, Impact and Seed**. As a Director he has devised and directed **Groundplay** for Blue Sky Arts and Media (London tour); **Beef** for the House of Talent at the Brady Arts Centre (London tour) and **Your Numbers Up** for the Round House Theatre Company (London and Edinburgh). Most recently he has directed **Fathers Inside** at Soho Theatre. As an Associate of Creative Learning at the National Youth Theatre he has created **Playing Up** which is a programme of study at level 3 (A-level) in Theatre Skills for young people not in education, training or employment.

He works as a trainer for **Youth at Risk** and **Leap Confronting Conflict**.

ALEX WALDMANN JOE

Alex trained at LAMDA.

Theatre includes: **Rope** (Almeida Theatre); **Hamlet, Twelfth Night** (Donmar Warehouse); **Troilus and Cressida** (Cheek by Jowl); **Angry Young Man** (Trafalgar Studios); **Hobson's Choice** (Chichester Festival); **Waltz of the Toreadors** (Chichester Minerva); **Macbeth** (West Yorkshire

Playhouse); **Big Love** (Gate Theatre); **Romeo and Juliet** (Birmingham REP Theatre); **Hortensia and the Museum of Dreams** (Finborough); **Fishbowl** (Theatre 503).
Film includes: **One-Eyed Chloe** and **The Eleventh Shot.**

JADE WILLIAMS PEARL

Theatre includes: **As You Like It, A New World – A Life of Thomas Paine** (Shakespeare's Globe Theatre); **Romeo and Juliet** (Shakespeare's Globe Theatre on Tour); **Piranha Heights** (Soho Theatre); **Chatroom/ Citizenship** (National Theatre/UK Tour and Hong Kong Festival); **I Like Mine With A Kiss** (Bush Theatre); **Market Boy** (National Theatre); **The Little Prince** (Hampstead Theatre); **Low Dat** (Birmingham Rep); **The Rise and Fall of Little Voice** (Harrogate Theatre); **Dark Of The Moon** (Kings Head); **Les Miserables** (Palace Theatre). Television includes: **Doctors, Holby City, EastEnders, Judge John Deed, The Canterbury Tales - The Pardoner's Tale, Serious And Organised** (Company Pictures); **William And Mary, The Bill** (Thames); **Mile High** (Hewlands for Sky); **Being April** (BBC); **Lloyd & Hill; Casualty, Other People's Children, The Sins, Hope & Glory, Bad Girls, Anything's Possible, Grange Hill, Wavelength, Plotlands,** and **Black Hearts in Battersea.**
Film includes: **Anne Frank, Hush Your Mouth** and **Life & Lyrics.** Radio includes: **Five Wedding Dresses, What Is She Doing Here?, The Day The Planes Came, Needle, Arcadia, The Family Man, The Third Trial, Birds, The Mother Of..., Reader for Secrets, Westway; Songs that Houses Sing, Up & Down in Silverton, A Handful of Dust, Voyage of the Dawntreader, The Silver Chair** and **Into The Mystic.**

NATASHA LANGRIDGE WRITER

Natasha Langridge founded Renegade this year. **Shraddhā** is its first production.
Natasha is co-author of **Rage and Reason: Women Playwrights on Playwriting** published by Methuen. She wrote and directed the tour of her one woman show, **Beverley**. After collecting stories about Brixton from its inhabitants she wrote and directed **Breathing in Brixton**, presented at The Oval House Theatre. With the dramaturgy of Bryony Lavery she wrote and directed **The Method**, performed Upstairs at The Oval House. Natasha is also an actress, most recently appearing in the Sanya Mihailovik film **Duties of a Lady Female**.
She trained at East 15 Acting School.

LISA GOLDMAN DIRECTOR

Lisa is the Artistic Director of Soho Theatre. Recently Lisa co-directed **Everything Must Go!**, a series of short works on the theme of economic crisis. Previous credits include: **This Isn't Romance** by In-Sook Chappell (winner of the Verity Bargate Award); **Piranha Heights** by Philip Ridley (nominated for Whatsonstage's Best Off-West End Production); **A Couple of Poor**, **Polish Speaking Romanians** by Dorota Maslowska (which she co-translated with Paul Sirett); **Baghdad Wedding** by Hassan Abdulrazzak (which she also directed as a Radio 3 Sunday play and which won the 2008 George Devine and Meyer-Whitworth awards for Best New Play); Lisa's first play with Soho Theatre was **Leaves of Glass**, also by Philip Ridley.

Previously as founding Artistic Director of the Red Room, Lisa developed and directed a huge body of radical new writing over 10 years. **Hoxton Story** was a site-specific walkabout piece, which she wrote and directed. Other new plays included **The Bogus Woman** (Fringe First, Bush/Traverse/tour/Radio 3 Sunday play), **Bites** (Bush Theatre), **Animal** (Soho Theatre) and **Hanging** (CBL Radio 4 play), all by Kay Adshead, **Playing Fields** by Neela Dolezalova (Soho Theatre Company), **Made In England** by Parv Bancil, **Sunspots**, **Know Your Rights** and **People On The River** all by Judy Upton, **Ex**, **Obsession** and **Surfing** (all Critic's Choice seasons at BAC) and a 35mm short film **My Sky Is Big** (NFT 1 and festivals), all by Rob Young. Lisa's long term producing collaboration with Anthony Neilson has enabled the creation of some of his finest work- she commissioned **The Censor** (Duke of York's) and **Stitching** (Bush Theatre), both Time Out Live Award winners, and also **The Night Before Christmas.**

JON BAUSOR DESIGNER

Jon read Music at Oxford University and Fine Art at Exeter College of Art before training on the Motley Theatre Design Course. He was a finalist in The Linbury Prize.

Theatre designs include **Big Love** (Abbey Theatre), **The Thief of Baghdad** (ROH), **The Birthday Party** (Lyric), **Romeo and Juliet**, **Julius Caesar** (Abbey Theatre, Dublin), **Terminus** (Peacock Theatre, Dublin/Public Theatre, New York), **Water** (Lyric/Filter tour), **Scenes From The Back of Beyond** (Royal Court), **The Soldier's Tale** (Old Vic), **James and the Giant Peach** (Octagon Theatre, Bolton, Best Production Winner Manchester Evening News Awards), **The Great Highway** (Gate Theatre, London), **Piranha Heights**, **Baghdad Wedding**, **Shrieks of Laughter** (Soho Theatre), **Direct Action season**, **The Soul Of Chien-nu** (Young Vic), **Carver** (Arcola), **Night time**, **In The Bag** (Traverse) and **Sanctuary** (National Theatre).

Dance includes **Scribblings** (Rambert), **Firebird** (Stadttheater, Bern) **Snow White In Black** (Phoenix Dance Theatre; Best Production, Dance Critics Circle award), **Echo and Narcissus**, **Before The Tempest** (Royal Opera House), **Ghosts** (Royal Opera House, London and Stadttheater, Bern) **Mixtures** (English National Ballet), **Non Exeunt** (George Piper Dances), and **Marjorie's World Unhinged** (Tilted/ tour). Opera design includes **The Knot Garden** (Klangbogen Festival, Vienna), **The**

Lighthouse (Teatro Poliziano, Montepulciano) and **The Queen of Spades** (Edinburgh Festival Theatre).

PHILIP GLADWELL LIGHTING DESIGNER

For Soho Theatre: **Overspill, HOTBOI** and **Tape**. Other shows include: **The Fahrenheit Twins** (Told by an Idiot); **Punk Rock** (Lyric Hammersmith); **2nd May 1997** (Bush); **Origins** (Pentabus); **Terminus** (Abbey & Tour); **Once on this Island** (Birmingham/Nottingham/Hackney); **After Dido** (English National Opera); **Macbeth** (Royal Exchange Manchester); **Harvest** (UK Tour); **Amazonia, Ghosts,** and **The Member of the Wedding** (Young Vic); **Oedipus Rex** (Royal Festival Hall); **Oxford Street** and **Kebab** (Royal Court); **Il Trittico** (Opera Zuid); **Testing the Echo** (Out Of Joint); **Falstaff** (Grange Park Opera); **Blithe Spirit & Black Comedy** (Watermill); **Drowning on Dry Land** (Salisbury Playhouse); **Melody** and **In the Bag** (Traverse); **Mother Courage** (Nottingham Playhouse/UK tour); **Into the Woods, Macbeth** and **Way Upstream** (Derby Playhouse); **The Bodies** (Live Theatre); **The Morris** (Liverpool Everyman); **Bread & Butter** (Tricycle); **Canterville Ghost** (Peacock); **Awakening** and **Another America** (Sadler's Wells).

MATT MCKENZIE SOUND DESIGNER

Matt came to the UK from New Zealand in 1978. He toured with Paines Plough before joining the Lyric Theatre Hammersmith in 1979, and then Autograph Sound in 1984. Theatre work includes: **Wuthering Heights** (Birmingham Rep); **Flamingos, Damages, After the End,** **tHedYsFUnCKshOnalZ** (Bush Theatre); **The Seagull, Master and Margarita, 5/11, Babes In Arms, Funny Girl, Music Man** (Chichester Festival Theatre); **Frame312, After Miss Julie and Days of Wine and Roses** (The Donmar); **Sweeney Todd, Merrily We Roll Along** (Derby Playhouse); **The Giant** (Hampstead); **Three Sisters on Hope Street** (Liverpool Everyman); **Angry Housewives, The Way of the World, Ghost Train** (Lyric Theatre Hammersmith); **Family Reunion, Henry V, Hamlet, The Lieutenant of Inishmore, Julius Caesar, A Midsummer Night's Dream, Indian Boy** (RSC); **Leaves of Glass, Baghdad Wedding** (Soho Theatre); **Iron, The People Next Door** (Traverse); **Made in Bangkok, The House of Bernarda Alba, A Piece of My Mind, Journey's End, A Madhouse in Goa, Gasping, Tango Argentino, When She Danced, Misery, Things We Do For Love, Long Day's Journey Into Night, Macbeth, Sexual Perversity in Chicago, A Life in the Theatre, Nicholas Nickleby** (West End); **Amadeus, Lysistrata, The Master Builder, School for Wives, A Streetcar Named Desire** (for Sir Peter Hall). He was also Sound Supervisor for the Peter Hall Seasons at The Old Vic and The Piccadilly and designed sound for **Waste, Cloud 9, The Seagull, The Provok'd Wife, King Lear, The Misnathrope, Major Barbara, Filumena,** and **Kafka's Dick**.

PERFORMANCE PROVOCATIVE AND
COMPELLING THEATRE, COMEDY AND CABARET
SOHO CONNECT A THRIVING EDUCATION,
COMMUNITY AND OUTREACH PROGRAMME
WRITERS' CENTRE DISCOVERING AND
NURTURING NEW WRITERS AND ARTISTS
SOHO THEATRE BAR OPEN UNTIL LATE
TICKET HOLDERS GET 10% OFF FOOD
AND DRINK

'The capital's centre for daring international drama.'
EVENING STANDARD

'A jewel in the West End.'
BBC LONDON

THE TERRACE BAR
Drinks can be taken into the auditorium and are available from
the Terrace Bar on the second floor.

SOHO THEATRE ONLINE
Giving you the latest information and previews of upcoming shows,
Soho Theatre can be found on facebook, myspace, twitter and youtube
as well as at sohotheatre.com

EMAIL INFORMATION LIST
For regular programme updates and offers visit sohotheatre.com/mailing

HIRING THE THEATRE
Soho Theatre and Soho Theatre Bar have a range of spaces for hire. Please
contact the theatre on 020 7287 5060 or go to sohotheatre.com/hires for
further details.

Soho Theatre is supported by
ACE, Bloomberg, TEQUILA\London,
Westminster City Council, The City Bridge Trust
Performances in the Lorenz Auditorium / Registered Charity No: 267234

THE SOHO THEATRE DEVELOPMENT CAMPAIGN

Soho Theatre receives core funding from Arts Council England, London. In order to provide as diverse a programme as possible and expand our audience development and outreach work, we rely upon additional support from trusts, foundations, individuals and businesses.

All of our major sponsors share a common commitment to developing new areas of activity and encouraging creative partnerships between business and the arts. We are immensely grateful for the invaluable support from our sponsors and donors and wish to thank them for their continued commitment.

Soho Theatre has a Friends Scheme in support of its education programme and work developing new writers and reaching new audiences.

To find out how to become a Friend of Soho Theatre, contact the development department on **020 7478 0111**, or visit **sohotheatre.com**

SHRADDHĀ

To the free spirit.

May it rise up, whatever happens.

First published in 2009 by Oberon Books Ltd
521 Caledonian Road, London N7 9RH
Tel: 020 7607 3637 / Fax: 020 7607 3629
e-mail: info@oberonbooks.com
www.oberonbooks.com

A catalogue record for this book is available from the British
Library.

ISBN: 978-1-84002-965-9

Cover photograph: Nigel Dickinson

Printed in Great Britain by CPI Antony Rowe, Chippenham

Introduction

I had just finished a production of my play, *The Method*, at The Oval House Upstairs and was feeling a bit depressed. I thought I should pull myself together so started to play with ideas for my next project. A loud voice in my head shouted GYPSIES, GYPSIES, GYPSIES! Maybe it was because I had been fascinated by the Romany heather sellers as a child. Or because I wanted to hear the Romany side of the story. Or because I felt like an outsider too, that I naively followed that voice, thinking I would go and find some English Romany people and chat to them. It took months before I found anyone who would talk to me or help me with my research. Many Romany people don't trust the gorgers (non-gypsies) and they can be difficult to find.

The sites Gypsies and Travellers live on are often located under flyovers, or on the edges of motorways or factories. They haven't chosen to live in these places. By law Gypsies and Travellers are only legally allowed to stop on these sites 'designated' by the local council. There are not enough designated sites provided, so many Travellers are forced to stop on land illegally (being moved on every few days) or to buy their own land (very expensive and difficult to get planning permission to live there) or to give up their traditional way of life and go into a house.

I asked everyone I had ever met if they knew any Romany people. A friend of a friend happened to be managing a young Romany girl singer and she and her mum graciously allowed me onto their site and into their spotlessly clean trailer in Hertfordshire over a few afternoons. I started to get an insight into their misunderstood culture and found opportunities to meet more of these warm-heated, hardworking and skilful people. I travelled to Appleby Horse Fair with Nathan who taught me some of the Romany language. I met Charlie in London who had grown up in poverty travelling with a horse-drawn vardo but, over time, made enough money to buy a house then knock it down in order to build a better one and to get around the laws that prevented his family and friends pulling up on his land in their trailers. I met Cliff in Norfolk while he was recovering from an eviction from his own land and the dispersion of his whole family. The first time I met Ann on her site in Essex she had just received a letter with 'Follow the smell' written under her designated site address. Another girl's wedding reception had been cancelled by the proprietors of the hall they had booked after he had found out that they were Travellers.

I met more Gypsies and I read books about their history and the constant persecution they have endured over the centuries. And I became increasingly enraged at the way this continues in modern England and Europe. It is quite acceptable in Romania for villagers to take torches into the Romany ghettos and burn their huts for sport. Here it still seems commonly acceptable to call Gypsies 'dirty, thieving pikeys'.

What struck me above all about the Romany people I met wasn't just their dignity, pride and survival skill but their strength of pure spirit. Something us gorgers seem to have lost. I sometimes felt the Romanies I met were the true humans. The rest of us mere automatons in a corporate reality.

As I attempted to start writing *Shraddhā*, after absorbing all this research, I heard about generations of Romany families being evicted from their site of forty years to make way for the 2012 Olympics. *Shraddhā* isn't a factual account of that eviction or what happened to those families. I wanted to use the Olympic eviction as a metaphor for the precarious existence our law-laden society has forced Romanies and Travellers to live.

And, of course, *Shraddhā* is a love story. Make of it what you will…

Natasha Langridge
October 2009

Characters

PEARL
A young Romany girl

JOE
A young gorger (house dweller) boy

ANN
A Romany woman and Pearl's Mum

GRANNY
A Romany woman and Ann's Mum

DEAN
A gorger man and Joe's Dad

SETTING
The play is set in East London and a wood in Sussex

THE TIME
2007 Summer

I would like to say thank you, primarily, to all the Romany people who gave me their stories, allowing me the privilege of seeing a little way into their world. Without your generosity Shraddhā *could not have been written. To Bryony Lavery, for her always beautiful and encouraging advice. To Ben and the Oval House for their support in* Shraddhā*'s early development. To Rebecca Gatward, for her loving direction of its first ever reading. To Lisa Goldman, for her amazing vision and* Shraddhā. *To Esther Richardson, for inspiration. To Nina Steiger for her brilliance and determination. To all at Soho for their hard work. And to my loyal friends and gorgeous, family – You know who you are!*

SCENE 1

A tatty silver fence

Joe is waiting behind it, smoking a roll up.
There is the sound of a washing machine.
Pearl comes out from that sound.
She stands a way back from the fence. He is right up at it.

JOE: How long have yer got?

PEARL: One load. Long spin

JOE: Come up here then

PEARL: Ye come here

JOE: I would if I could

PEARL: Would ye?

JOE: Be over the top like one of them high jumpers

PEARL: What?

JOE: Sportsmen

PEARL: I know what one is and ye's not it. Get stuck up on the top

JOE: Come closer and I'll show you me muscles

PEARL: Take ye top off I can see from 'ere

JOE: Shut up

PEARL: Need a magnifying glass would I?

JOE: I saw you today. In the shopping centre. With those girls.
And a baby

PEARL: Me sisters. The eldest one's little chavvy

JOE: Not yours?

PEARL: I'm not married! I told ye that

JOE: So?

PEARL gives him a don't you dare look.

Where you gonna go?

He waits for an answer that doesn't come.

When the Games come?

PEARL: Council want us pull onto that playground they nicked from that estate up the way

JOE: You gonna?

PEARL: We don't wanna

JOE: Where then?

PEARL: Dunno

JOE: With me?

PEARL looks away.

I'll follow you

PEARL: Ye won't know where

JOE: You'll tell me

PEARL: I won't know where

JOE: I do

PEARL: Yeah?

JOE: With me

PEARL: Me brother came back with one of yourn last night

JOE: How do you know that?

PEARL: Heard 'em in the trailer

JOE: So?

PEARL: Ours wouldn't.
Wouldn't make that sound like…

JOE: Like what?

PEARL: You don't know like what?

JOE: How would I?

She gives him a I'm not stupid look.

I never felt till I saw you

PEARL: He uses 'em for practice

JOE: I never felt. Truly

PEARL: Truly? That's a funny word for it

JOE: Come up here

PEARL: Come over 'ere

JOE: OK. I will

He starts to climb.

PEARL: What are ye doing?

JOE: I'm coming over

PEARL: Get down

JOE: No

PEARL: Get down!

JOE: Come closer then

PEARL: Stop. They'll see ye

JOE: I don't care

PEARL: Ye will when they catch ye

JOE: Only one way to stop me

PEARL: SSSsssssh. No higher. Too high!

JOE: Shit. I can see them
They can see me

He jumps down.

PEARL: Stupid fecking twat

JOE: Kiss me

Spin cycle goes into noisy overdrive.

PEARL: They're coming

JOE: Kiss me

PEARL: Go…… (*Kisses him.*) ……………don't come morrow

They start moving apart.

JOE: When?

PEARL: Friday…………morn…early

JOE: You taste of petals

PEARL: Twat…early

He runs.

SCENE 2

Inside the trailer

30 minutes later.

Sound of construction work in background.

ANN is making sandwiches.
PEARL comes in.

ANN: Ye get lost?

PEARL: Got stuck on no 3. Had to drain it and start again

Starts polishing up a series of Waterford glass.

It's all hung up

ANN: Fer it
All te get covered in dust from them diggers

PEARL: Hung it on other side frem 'em

ANN: Won't be no other side soon

PEARL: Where's the chavvies?

ANN: Kelly's taken them to the shop

PEARL: That'll be a first. Without me to carry 'em back
How she get little Davy boy to go? Without me?

ANN: Ice cream

22

PEARL: Did ye tell her to go to Sainsbury's cos they don't have the one he likes anywhere else

ANN: She knows her own son

PEARL: She don't know that. He's always round here daytime

ANN: He asked for ye. Kelly says ye'd be waiting for him when they come back

PEARL: Where else am I gonna be?

Pause.

How's Davy boy's dreams last night?

ANN: Still bad. Wake up crying

PEARL: (*Shouts out of trailer.*) That close it was.
Like being in starry all of us can't even let the chavvies play out case they gets run down by bleedin tractor
The races 'aven't started yet ye know

ANN: They can't hear ye.
Goes on like this won't be able te hear them

She takes packet of pills out of cupboard.

Be bleedin deaf.
Solve one problem

PEARL: Ye took half a packet afore this morning

ANN: If doctor give me stronger ones wouldn't need te take so many

PEARL gently turns her away from pills.

PEARL: I'll do sandwiches. Ye have a rest

ANN: Need more than a bleedin rest take this pain away

PEARL takes over the sandwiches.

PEARL: Think about something else

ANN: Ye hands are shakin

PEARL: Can't help it. Makes me wanna kill

ANN: Watch what ye doin with that knife then

23

Pause.

ANN: Clive boy phoned early. While ye was with that gorger boy

PEARL freezes.

PEARL: I wasn't with…

What did they do to him?

ANN: Not harmed him

PEARL: I was only talking

ANN starts polishing a figurine.

ANN: What if Clive boy got to hear it?

PEARL: How will he?

ANN: It won't get no further. Long as it don't go no further

PEARL: What did they do to him?

ANN: How'd that mochady gorger boy ever git a living te keep ye?

PEARL: We was only talking

ANN: Did he say loved ye?

PEARL: No!

ANN: Do ye love him?

PEARL: How can I love him?

ANN: Ye can't if ye know what's good for ye

PEARL: We was only talking!

ANN: He won't come back

PEARL: What did they do to him?

ANN: Just rocker with him. Nice and quiet. What he was about. What he wanted. What he got

PEARL: He didn't get nothing

ANN: And he ain't gonna cos he's got nothing to give ye

PEARL: He was charmin' to me

ANN: Clive 'ull be charming to ye an he'll give ye something ta live on an all

PEARL: He was brave

ANN: Where is he then?

Pause.

Ye ain't gonna forget ye self are ye?

PEARL finishes sandwiches and takes a figurine.

PEARL: Where's Granny?

ANN: On the internet with Alice. Looking at them pictures of Wayne and Colleen's wedding

PEARL: 'She did look handsome'

ANN: Ye never in ye life walked down the bleedin' street on ye own. How did ye's meet him?

PEARL: He was just there one day……on the path…behind the fence

ANN: How did he get there?

PEARL: Been running from something…breathless

ANN: She wants ye's to be grander. Three truck loads of white roses we can get ye. Makes me wanna get married all over again

PEARL: He looked at me and he didn't move.
I went in the washing hut and I never looked out of the window
I stayed in there till it had finished

ANN: They've got a good business up there. Clive boy 'ull be able te get ye a separate little kitchen trailer. Pink

PEARL: Though I knows he isn't but he looks more like one of us than

ANN: They got a plot big enough fer ye's te stop on. Permanent. Won't be no games going there. Up Norfolk way. You'll be safe Pearl

PEARL: He said I must have diamonds in the back of me eyes cos he never seen any light up so

ANN: Can he match 'em with ones he can put on ye finger?

PEARL: I never went close up to the fence. Never too close. Never. I'm clean. He never touched me. I'm still clean and decent. Just like I was before

Pause.

ANN: I never seen a smile so big on ye face as when ye first set ye yox on Clive boy. Ye's was six year old and he were seven. Up at Violet's wedding. Ye remember

PEARL: He stroked me hair then kissed it. 'Like treasure', he said

ANN: That's how it'll be with him. Like treasure

PEARL starts polishing a figurine.

(*Puts figurine down.*) Did he kiss ye? That gorger boy?

PEARL: He never touched me

ANN: Did he kiss ye?

PEARL: No. He never kissed me (*Puts figurine down.*)

SCENE 3

The fence

The next morning.

PEARL: I told ye not te come today.
Ye's lucky ye still standing

JOE: Can't keep away from yer

PEARL: Quickwash. They'll be timing it

JOE: Come here then

PEARL: I'm betrothed. I told ye that first time

JOE: Didn't stop you though did it?

PEARL: I'm getting married

JOE: Even after

PEARL: I'm marrying him

JOE: Why?

PEARL: He deserves me

JOE: An I don't?

PEARL: He loves me
fer real

JOE: Cos he's a Romany? That him makes him real do it?

PEARL: Makes him true.
Loved him all me life

JOE: Kissed him?

PEARL: He give me the most special thing a Romany can give

JOE: What?

PEARL: The most beautiful song he could

JOE: I'll give yer a song Pearl

PEARL: Not like that!
It be
so special
so
most beautiful
so
dazzling
That if a Romany man give it te a woman
Or a Romany woman give it te a man
It will bind that loved one to 'em whoever they be
The song be like ropes o love golden and strong forever and ever

JOE: What is that song Pearl?

PEARL: It's got secrets in it
And magic
I can't sing it te thee or no one.
It's just fer me
Frem him

JOE: I'll sing yer a better one

27

PEARL: Won't work Joe
Ye's not a Romany
Though ye'd like te be
Never will

JOE: I love ye greater than him

PEARL: How does ye know that?

JOE: Pearl I'm here. Where is he?

PEARL: With his family. Ready and waiting fer me

JOE: If he loved yer he'd come and get yer

PEARL: He's been here te ask fer me.
He's just waiting fer me te say when

JOE: Come here

PEARL: I can't Joe. His song holds me to him. Like his arms be
round me every minute o the day

JOE: They weren't when ye kissed me

PEARL: I were just seeing
what a gorger tasted like

JOE: Must have liked it. Or ye wouldn't be standing here now

PEARL: Just saying goodbye. While I git me washing done. All the
lamp-posts here been dug up They've even rerouted the buses Joe.
You'll forget and I'll be married

JOE: You'll always feel me Pearl. And you'll always wonder
what life with the gorger boy might have been like

PEARL: What would it be like?

JOE: I can't see the future. I'm not a Romany

She waits then whispers.

PEARL: If someone else does something ever so brave or ever so
beautiful the song Clive boy give me can be broken

JOE: And if I give ye something ever so brave or ever so beautiful
what will you give me?

She waits.

PEARL: How brave and how beautiful is it?

SCENE 4

Sound of horses racing on concrete

Next day. Morning.

JOE is standing alone. Exhilarated.

JOE: Anything can happen at Appleby fair

Wild

On that path. Before. Back there. In London. Her daddy's eyes. Her brothers eyes. Blocked my path. Out of their site. Told me, moungst some other things, they weren't never ever forever gonna put any Shraddhā in me

But I got here.
Up the motorway
to Cumbria
With me idea
An' I got something arranged.
Gonna make 'em see
I have got something
to give her
Gotta follow that man – that (*Corrects himself with relish.*) 'Rom' –
the big man –
Over the river

Shit.
Bare-chested chavvies leading stallions past
the wide chested men with special shiny twisted sticks pulling
ten Shetlands past the girls – the – 'raklis' – with boots caps and
earrings coming out with brown eyed piebalds
onto the verge
Muddy
'Andsome man – 'mush' they call 'em – on his mobile up skewbald
mare with her foal running behind cuts

through and down into the lathered water to fairy liquid wash
and shine into the crescent of the river full of more horses horses
horses –'grai'.
'Mind the way'
I do.
Up the hill.
Girls – raklis – in skirts up to here and too high heels to walk in
pushing babies in buggies sucking
solid gold dummies laughing as the eight year old boy passes on the
back of a black
stallion reigns in one hand fag in the other
faster
faster
gettttttttt!
Under the bridge more Shetlands tied up together another
over there a few brown
and white mares tethered chewing up the grass
RSPCA walking like sore thumbs around looking over their
shoulder
won't find much to do here.
Too much money in them horses – in them 'grai'
Had to climb through
huddled crowded round weren't gonna let me see
'I'll give ye five
I'll give ye five and a half
I'll give ye six
I'll give ye six
I'll give ye six
I'll give ye six and a half
Go on ye don't want te take it home with ye
I'll give ye six and a half
I'll give ye seven
Done'

Same grai sold three times in that hour

Come onto first field.
Stalls of mink hair bands and Harrods cups.
Old saddles.
Fortune tellers havin a fag on a rest.

Chanel cushions. Old kettle pots. Photo's of last years fair '
Look that's aunty Diane and Jimmy boy.'
Diamonds
look at that
and gold and cash cash cash-'dosh.'
A boy with his girl drops some but I don't risk it, not gonna need it,
if I can find this Rom
around here somewhere.
At the back he said
Walk through trucks and more
grai
grai
grai tied up to the sides when one starts they all go
calling
the warm breath gets up a wind touches my face.
Raklis' stilettos stick in the mud dunno how she walks.
Better than me.
Then I hear it
muted roars, further back.
Past the old wagon's painted gold and green.
See mushes's heads coming up from behind
the top of a truck and bodies swaying out from the side
I know that must be one.
I move closer.
All the mush leaning tight in.
Chavvies standing on shoulders.
No way in for me.
Others hanging off the roof. My heart is buckling inside me. Then
they all move down.
Bodies in closer and further to the ground.
And
They're up.
Can see the ones in the middle all cut up. ' Let's have a drink and
that'll be that.' Shake hands and off they go. Arms round to keep
each other up.
I move in

The Rom who arranged it, who I persuaded to arrange it down on
the river cos he looked like the sort who could, he looks at me with
a smile while he shouts
'Who's gonna start on the gorger?' And gets some answers

'Ain't much of 'im.'
Brave little runt though.'
'Takin' me on.'
I knew he'd done the circuits and I ain't never not without gloves
and rounds But I must be able and they start at a tenner. Then more
joined and both sides are taking money
and I thought about the diamond I was gonna get her thought about
having her all night thought about the light deep in the back of her
eyes and I looked at the boy standing
opposite me
lightweight like me
hungry like me
all his people around him
not like me
and the Rom who'd arranged it who thought it was funny when
I first asked him who
thought I couldn't take it
who thought I was out of my depth said, ' May the best mush win'
and I knew that was me.
And I hit him the boy square in the centre of his chin he didn't have
time to recover I
laid another into his cheek and felt a pain raw in me knuckles but it
got took away with a jab to the nose felt it crack. I wobbled back but
thought of her lips and stepped forward swiped at him missed he
got me in the side on the temple blood already spurting didn't know
whether it was his or mine.
'Have ye had enough little gorger?'
I thought of her hair falling on my face
stepped forward and cracked him right up the nose
heard it go.
Both of us now.
Couldn't hear what they was saying. Just noise now.
Move your fucking feet inside of me said. Got to give him the run
round. Pick 'em up.
Heavy now. But brought him round and looked him square on and
saw he had something that wasn't part of me saw animal in him
I had lost.
Pure instinct raw desire nothing complicated force of nature life
survival.
Needed it now

Can taste the salt in my mouth the sweat and the blood thought
about tickling the creases between her toes
my heart is shouting get the fuck out
'He's going down'
I can hear that
No
And I fucking hit him
Crack crack crack
I fucking hit him over and over and over didn't give him a chance
didn't care whose fucking brother or son or cousin he was he's
putting himself there and I gotta win go down you cunt go down I
shout he's wobbly and I can feel it coming taste triumph on my lips
I'm gonna beat the fucker the one they said I never could I'm gonna
beat him into the ground I'm gonna win that money take it back to
London and make them see

*His head and body move back as if he's taken a forceful punch and he falls
to the ground.*

Blackout.

SCENE 5

Joe and Dean's council flat

Late that night.

DEAN is putting disinfectant on JOE's cuts.

DEAN: You haven't been in the ring for a year what you doing
fighting fucking pikeys?

JOE: I was gonna win

DEAN: You only ever won one fucking match and that was cos the
other geezer was half pissed before he started

JOE: I was gonna win

DEAN: Fucking animals. Look at you.
Keep still

JOE: They brought me a pint and a sandwich after

DEAN: With the dosh they won on you? Stupid little cunt. Go all the
way to Cumbria to get smashed up.
Keep still will you

JOE: It hurts

DEAN: Go down the post office tomorrow. You don't need no
qualifications for that

JOE: Do you know what they get paid?

DEAN: Better than nothing

JOE: Not to wear that uniform

DEAN: Is it a girl? Is that what's got you?

JOE: No

DEAN: It is isn't it?

JOE: No

DEAN: A pikey girl? Here? In London?

JOE: No

DEAN: Jesus fucking Christ. Do they know where you live?

JOE: They're not like that

DEAN: Who did this to you then?

JOE: It weren't them. I told you. Not the ones down here not
her family. This was an arranged fight I arranged it at the fair in
Cumbria. Appleby. And they're not pikeys. They're Romanies.
Originally from India. A thousand years ago

DEAN: Fucking Paki Pikeys.
Where did you learn that?

JOE: I heard it on the radio

DEAN: When do you listen to the radio?

JOE: When you're at work

DEAN: Glad you're doing something useful then. Gonna be a
fucking pikey historian are you?

JOE: Ouch

DEAN: That's it now. There's no infection.
You'll still have your pretty face.
You haven't got her up the duff ave yer?

JOE: I never touched her

DEAN: So what you fighting for then?

JOE: I wanted to buy her something

DEAN: Get a fucking job then!

JOE: I wanna get an horse

DEAN: You wanna fucking what?

JOE: I wanna buy an horse. I can get one for 250 quid. Will you
lend it me? Please? Please?

DEAN: What you gonna do with a fucking horse?

JOE: Sell it. For more than I bought it

DEAN: Where you gonna keep it?

JOE: On the grass at the back

DEAN: How am I gonna explain that to the council?

JOE: It won't be for long

DEAN: What you gonna do with the money?

JOE: Buy another one. I'll be an horse dealer

DEAN: Keep an herd of 'em round the back will yer?

JOE: Get 'em some hay and…

DEAN: Where you gonna get hay round ere? In Hackney?

JOE: Pet shop

DEAN: Might get enough for a couple of rabbits

JOE: Some of 'em go for thirty grand

DEAN: Where you gonna get thirty grand?

JOE: I could keep one in the sheds down there

DEAN: Yeah, then you wouldn't have to worry about what to feed it. The crack heads could pass it the pipe
(*Does impression of a horse on crack.*)

JOE: I could start with a small one. A Shetland. Keep it in here and ride it out at night

DEAN: When you ever rode an horse?

JOE: It's to groom up

DEAN: You don't know how

JOE: There's books you can get

DEAN: You can barely read

JOE: I can read enough for that

DEAN: Go to fucking college then and do something normal

JOE: You don't get any money at college

DEAN: You haven't got any fucking money now

JOE: That's why I'm asking you for some

DEAN: What's she got ay? A diamond studded cunt?

SCENE 6

The fence

Next morning.

The washing machine can be heard.

JOE and PEARL are close up either side of the fence – but not quite touching it. His face is still bruised.

PEARL: He was a boxer

JOE: Yer Granddad was a proper one. An' an horse dealer. I know. I wouldn't run off and leave yer though

PEARL: They wouldn't let him keep his grai here

JOE: I wouldn't care where we was long as…

PEARL: That's cos ye got no grai

JOE: I got other things though

PEARL: Yeah?
What?

JOE: I got you. You're like a grai. Pride on legs that's you

PEARL: Was there any in the pub?

JOE: Na – just signs saying 'No Horses Inside.'
Lots tied up outside on the posts of the tea rooms and that

PEARL: Was there songs inside?

JOE: Yeah an' in the hotel

PEARL: Ye went in the hotel at Appleby Fair?

JOE: Yeah

PEARL: How did ye…

JOE smiles.

Did ye do a turn?

JOE: Yeah

PEARL: Let's 'ave it then

He looks down.

What gone shy?

He shifts about.

That's how they met. He done a song and she done a poem. They danced and he asked for her hand. She said no but they had another dance and then they went off got te Gretna Green

JOE: Must have been a good dance then

PEARL: He was an 'andsome Romany Rai and…

JOE: And where is he now?

PEARL: Travelling. (*Rolls her eyes.*) He's a traveller

JOE: Not like yer then

PEARL: Fuck off

JOE: Yer never bin nowhere. Never bin off this site.
Never been out of London

PEARL: I

JOE: 'Bin to that hotel in Spain'

PEARL: Fucking mochady gorger

JOE: I ain't mochady

PEARL: Ye are and useless too

JOE: Smell me yer'll see how clean I am.
Come over here I'll show yer how useless I am

PEARL: Alright then (*She pushes herself up against fence.*)

JOE looks startled.

Alright then (*She starts climbing fence.*)

JOE: Go any higher they'll see yer

She stops. Then takes another small step up.

Go any further there's no going back

She goes to take another step up. Waits.

It's…

She lets go and falls to ground. Lands on her feet.

PEARL: Ye all mouth and no strides.
Fucking wannabe

JOE looks at her – lost.

Ye don't know nothing

JOE: I know how much that diamond was

PEARL: How?

JOE: Two an a half

PEARL: Could have brought it for two sold it for three later
at Wisbech

JOE: If I'd won

PEARL: Was there all grai in that dip in the big field at the side?

JOE: Weren't no dip. Most tied up to trucks. End of day some was
banging their heads 'gainst it

PEARL: Didn't used to be like that

JOE: How do yer know? Ain't never bin

PEARL: I ain't a Romany girl for nothing

JOE: Touch me fingers Pearl

She waits. Then touches his fingers. Then his face.

PEARL: Me Great, Great Granny Coulson, me Granny's
Granny, who lived in the forest, had a leather belt with all stones
and buttons in.
The story stones.
That she always keep round her waist on her belt

When the chavvies asked for a story sitting round the fire.
In the forest. At night.
'Tell us a story Granny. Tell us a story.'
She'd look in the belt –at all the stones and buttons and say, 'which
one of you is it today,' she'd take one out and tell its story

Never told the same story twice

She said the stone would tell her its story.
But she wouldn't let the chavvies touch 'em. Not ever

She was sleeping one afternoon cos she was old but still do a bit of
hawking with her heather basket at the doors and if she got an in a
palm or two as well.
So she lay down under her canvas and had a kip.
Me own Granny
whose daddy would go the sea to play fiddle to the seals
they'd all come up to listen cos they loved that music in their hearts.
Well, she and one of her sisters
sneaked quiet as under her canvas and ever so sssh pulled the wallet
up from under her nose what was snoring and out round the back
of the tent so no one else could know. They peak in it to dick if the
stones would talk to 'em cos they was only eight and six year old.

After checking it was just like it were when they found it – that all the stones and all the buttons was in the same places they ssssh took it back under her nose that was still snoring and sneaked out again.

After they had their their stew that night all the chavvies were,
'Tell us a story Granny, tell us'
She lit her pipe ever so slow then looked in her wallet,' Sorry I can't. Someone has opened this wallet and all the stories have gone, 'cept one'
And she never told them another story again. Not ever

JOE: Bit mean init?

PEARL: Me Granny say she ever so careful what she dick into since. She say ye must never pry into magic ye gotta leave it te itself else ye disturb its nature and if ye do that…ye could make this heaven into an hell

JOE: What was the last story ? Did your Granny's Granny ever tell anyone ? What was it?

PEARL: I can't tell ye that

JOE: Why not?

PEARL: I ain't never given a gorger a story afore. Why should I give the last one te thee?

JOE: You don't know what it is do yer?

PEARL: You'll never find out will ye?
Unless…

JOE: What?

PEARL looks away.

Look at me Pearl!

She does.

PEARL: It ain't enough

No

JOE: What do I have te?

PEARL: Something braver

JOE: Braver!

PEARL: It's stopped. Gotta go. They'll come looking

She goes into washing hut.

JOE: When shall I come?

Couple of days?
When then?

She comes out of hut and looks at him turns and goes.

Lights fade on JOE.

SCENE 7

Inside the trailer

Five minutes later.

GRANNY LOVERIDGE is sewing a patchwork quilt.

PEARL comes in. She starts making sandwiches.

GRANNY: Ye seen him agin?

PEARL: No

GRANNY: Ye look like the wind slapped ye face.
They won't let ye do the washing any more

PEARL: I won't cry over that.
What shall I give 'em today? Cheese and ham or ham and pickle
and cheese an onion or ham and cheese?

GRANNY: Don't think they'll mind what arrangement ye give 'em
their vittals in – after all that landscaping be pleased just te feed the
howling in their bellies
(*Laughing.*) Trouble with nowadays. Have te feed ye men

PEARL: Got no hotchi hedgehog fat to smear round their lips when
they drunk and sleeping

GRANNY: Wake up, 'Where's me dinner?'

PEARL: You've had it. Can't ye taste it?

41

Picks up sandwich.

Ye want one?

GRANNY: No but I'll have a cuppa tea with ye

PEARL puts sandwich in her mouth and the kettle on.

What's he look like?

PEARL: Can't remember

GRANNY gives her a I weren't born yesterday look.

I only saw him there a couple of times. Behind the fence. He weren't nothing

GRANNY: That why he left ye that rose in the fence?

PEARL: He never

GRANNY: It were an old sort and fat. Red

PEARL: I never saw that

ANN comes in moving fast.

ANN: Poor rackli's shakin. They bin driving round the motorway for two day. Round and round. Couldn't find nowhere to stop.
Got shifted off own land.
Gave 'em some parni and made 'em cup of tea. Chavvies look like someone chored their spirits away. Their daddy got a brick in his face. Stopped fer a rest on the hard shoulder… Passers by chucked it through the window.
Gave 'em some of Davy boy's biscuits

GRANNY: What name?

ANN: Todd

GRANNY: From over Kent way?

ANN: Mm (*Eats sandwich.*)

GRANNY: Used to meet up with that family apple picking. They shared their dinners with us when we didn't have nothing. Had a son. What were his name? Tom. Tom boy. He chored a chicken when we had no meat to go with our tatties but he couldn't kill it. Couldn't get a grip. It were a slippery bugger.

Ye's granddaddy wrung its neck.
How long they been on it?

ANN: Five year. Council wouldn't new that planning bleedin'
permission for

GRANNY: 'em te keep their trailers on

ANN: Their own land

GRANNY: Like Lorraine and Alfie boy

ANN: Scrimped and saved fer ten year te buy that land

GRANNY: Like paradise Alfie boy say it were. All cousins playing
together. Four grandparents there. All the uncles and aunties.
Could go off travelling come back not lost yer plot.
Let others pull up on it too. Use it as an atchin tan.
An no one to stop 'em having yog at night

PEARL: Lorraine say it were a wonderful thing. The blazing yog
and the singsong

ANN: Where she is now has to hose the trailer down twice a day te
shift the black coming off the motorway above and the muck from
that factory at the side

GRANNY: And there be a waiting list to stop there

ANN: Under a bleedin' flyover

PEARL: Should I make some more fer 'em?

ANN: Yeah

PEARL makes more sandwiches.

GRANNY: Del mandi ye yox fer this needle

ANN goes to her to thread the needle.

Lorraine be on the valium now

ANN: Wakes up te rats in the bins. Won't give 'em any wheelies

PEARL: I wanna come with ye. When they come

ANN: Ye wanna marry Clive boy. Have a decent life. Like ye were
brought up te

43

ANN starts cleaning the mirrors.

GRANNY: She fading fer Clive boy

ANN: She like im at Arthur's funeral

GRANNY: Those grai were grand

ANN: Eyes all down each other over Shelley's wedding cake

GRANNY: He fancy ye strong. Wanna treat ye like a Queen

ANN: Feel like a Queen in the bed with him. He be a cushti dicken mush kai

Say you're ready and he'll come te ask fer thee

GRANNY: Afore he goes bald an ye get fat

ANN: Take ye te the pictures

GRANNY: I'll be chaperone

PEARL: Why can't I come with ye?

ANN: Ye gen dinlow !
Ye can't do better than im.
Life he give ye. Ye never gonna be on side of the road

GRANNY: Verges gone

ANN: Never have the gavvers knocking ye door down with enforcement orders not giving you time for a cup or git ye chavvies dressed in the snow before ye got te go not knowing where ye going driving round the motorways for hours feeling cushti bok if ye get a car park te stop for a couple of days

Ye chavvies won't have te go te different school every month cos always in a different place. Have te prove yeself every time

GRANNY: Come home from school te find the trailer gone

ANN: Clive boys gonna give ye better than what ye had here before. Without no Games coming te shift ye off. Not up in Norfolk. Peace and quiet there. Even room te build a kennel fer yer jukels

GRANNY: An an heart te paint it pink

ANN: Taps on every plot not one cold thing for the whole mumpley
site to wash ye hair in
Some so poor can't afford a generator for light
Concrete above keeping the sun from ye

GRANNY: Pearl never had te see her Mummy crying cos she can't
go on and the men come with their crane and lift your trailer
and everything in it all the china and glass crashing to nothing
everything she ever had

ANN: Say ye ready Pearl afore we get shifted

PEARL: Packin and unpackin. Eleven times already

GRANNY: Or buried under them bleedin' Games

PEARL: Maybe that day be far off

GRANNY: That day be as far off as them cranes an that iron wall
they bring with 'em when they've dug up all life in front of 'em

ANN: If we'd won that appeal might 'ave stood a chance

GRANNY: But we didn't
An' lawyer say we got five day te jell

Pearl? Does ye want te de what the council bid us an stop on the
playground they stole from the gorger kids?

ANN: Live there with their mummy and daddies' agitation
every day?

GRANNY: Or go out on the drom?
Like it be now?

ANN: All fer a bleedin pool they be buildin here

GRANNY: Fer seventeen days o synchronized swimming

GRANNY and ANN stare at PEARL.

PEARL: I'll get them crumbs up

Gets the Hoover out.

ANN: I'll take these up

Picks one plate of sandwiches up and goes.

PEARL Hoovers up
for a bit.
then
stops.
Turns it off.

Silence
as
PEARL arranges cups and plates.

PEARL: Where ye gonna go Granny? When we ave te?

GRANNY: Don't be fretting 'bout me. I'm too wicked fer God
te take me yet

I'll follow us destiny.
Like ye will

And that ain't with no wannabe gorger walking straight into a
curse o shame and taking all ye's people with ye
Ye'll phone Clive boy in the morning and tell 'im te start make plans
And this quilt be put to its proper use

Stands to hold quilt up. PEARL takes other side.

Sound of men's trucks.

Lights fade.

SCENE 8

Joe is revealed outside the trailer

That night.

The lights and a TV are on.

JOE: I'm sorry to disturb yer… Mrs Penfold… Mr Penfold

Sound of dogs barking.

I had to come

Back

I had to

46

I know what yer said about what you'd do to me teeth
but
I've come to ask yer
to your face

Straight

Can I come in?

Will you come out?

I know what yer said before 'bout me knees
But if yer knew what was in me
Please
Give me a go to win your daughter's heart
I know I ain't rich
I know I ain't all the things I gotta be
But I can learn
If yer show me
Yer ways
Teach me how you do it
I never had no one to teach me
It ain't my fault I was born a gorger
I'll work harder than you even
I'll work and work and work
till I'm *it*
Please
Give me a go

Please answer me

I ain't goin' away

I can't
I was just dragging around in the dark before
No light
Anywhere

But in her

Brightness
Life like I never seen

Please
What can I do?

I gotta have it

Gets on his knees.

Her

Tell me an I'll do it

I'll do it

Please

He waits for a long time.
More and more dogs are barking.

SCENE 9

Joe on the doorstep of his flat

Same night.

JOE is in his underpants. He is staggeringly pissed. DEAN opens the door.

DEAN: Where's yer fucking keys?

Pulls him into sitting room.

They've nicked yer fucking pockets.
Shit.
How did yer get home?

JOE: In a truck

DEAN: Now they know where yer fucking live don't they?
Have to get the fucking locks changed another 80 quid Jesus
fucking Christ almighty

JOE: They wouldn't want our tat. Got big silver flat screens and
everything

DEAN: Cos they're thieving pikeys

JOE: They work. Just for themselves

DEAN: : Yeah probably selling your Doctor Martens for twice what
yer paid for 'em

JOE: I didn't pay nothing for 'em

DEAN: Surprised they brought yer back then.
You'd fit in well with them

DEAN gives him a dressing gown.
He puts it on the wrong way round.

JOE: I never nicked nothing from you

DEAN: Yer don't pay me no fucking rent though do yer?

JOE: Yer wouldn't need it if you hadn't got that stupid mortgage.
For this dump.
Should've stayed paying rent on it. Wasn't that much.
They pay more on the site for a plot to put their trailer on

DEAN: Get benefit to pay it though don't they

JOE: No. Not all of 'em. I told yer

DEAN: Why don't yer get a job off them then?

JOE: They won't give me one……
Ain't got the skills they need. Don't know about trees or cars or
scrap or building or tarmacing or landscaping or cars

DEAN: Or horses

JOE: 'Can't keep a wife through petty choring'

DEAN: Not even good enough for the pikeys

Gives him some water.

JOE: I drank as much as them though
Passed that test.
Eighteen pints without throwing up

If I go back. They'll batter me head in.
With a bat.

I wanna die

DEAN: Like the time you wanted that hamster. You got over that.
You'll get over her

JOE finding it hard to drink the water down.

JOE: Give me some of that stuff

49

DEAN: What stuff?

JOE: The stuff you take before you go to work

DEAN: I dunno what you're talking about

JOE: I know where you keep it. I seen you do it

DEAN: It's only occasional

JOE: Getting more and more though isn't it?

DEAN: You try doing two fucking jobs. You can't even do one

Goes to kitchen, comes back with speed and paraphernalia in a biscuit tin.

JOE: You wouldn't need two jobs if you didn't have that stupid mortgage

DEAN: I got it so I'd have something to leave you Joe

JOE: You got it to make yerself feel better bout doing a job you hate

DEAN: Everybody hates their jobs

JOE: That's why I ain't got one

DEAN: That's why I've got two

JOE: Sell it then. If it was for me. Sell it and give us half the money

DEAN: I have (*Snorts a line, pushes it over to JOE.*)

JOE: You what?

DEAN: I'm going to live in Bulgaria. It's sorted

JOE: What are you gonna do there?

DEAN: Nothing. I'm gonna do nothing. With my friend

JOE: What friend?

DEAN: A friend

JOE: Which one?

DEAN: You never met her

JOE: Why not?

DEAN: Cos you were always rude to 'em

JOE: They changed so fast I never got a chance to be rude to 'em
(*Snorts line.*)

DEAN: I'm not just yer Dad Joe. I am a man. Got a right to a life

JOE: How much you gonna give me?

DEAN: I ain't dead yet

JOE: Where am I gonna live?

DEAN: Don't sound like it'll be on the pikey site

JOE: They're being chucked off anyway

DEAN: 'Bout time

You'll have te get a job won't yer. Get a room somewhere.
I've done me best. I've looked after yer and…

JOE: Didn't have to

DEAN: No I didn't. But I did. I put a roof over our heads I fed
and clothed yer

JOE: That's about all yer did do

DEAN: I had to go to work to keep us
Do yer think I liked it?
Na…yer don't ever think about me…do yer?
Getting up day after day year after year…
Tryin to set yer an example

JOE: They laugh at us you know. Wage slaves they call us. Get up
go to work to make somebody else rich come home watch the telly
go to bed get up and on and on and on

DEAN: Let 'em laugh. I ain't the one being chucked out me home

JOE: Give us some of the money. I'll be a property developer.
They said if I was rich enough to buy an house and knock it down
I could marry her. I could marry 'em all

DEAN: What they wanna knock it down for?

JOE: Build a better one. Have all their family pull onto the land in
their trailers. No one can get 'em off then

DEAN: Pikeys in the garden. All run round naked do they?

JOE: I took 'em off. I was hot

DEAN: What were yer doing?

JOE: Dancing

DEAN: And they weren't impressed enough to give yer their daughter?

JOE: I'll kill meself

DEAN: Not with that yer won't (*Pulls biscuit tin closer.*)

JOE: Yer a cunt

DEAN: And you're homeless

SCENE 10

Pearl is at the top of the fence. Her side

Just before dawn next morning.

PEARL climbs over and halfway down then drops. Lands on her feet. The fence disappears. She walks on. Low light.

PEARL: The Drom

Look forward

Nix is different

Buildings

Cars

Walking

Straight
To the end
Then left
Then right

Think of Granny walking.
Feel her basket heavy on my arm

The light is coming up proper

Precinct

Shutters down

Past Primark, Next, Sainsbury's Local, Abbey, Woolworths,
Haart Estates, past Greggs the baker, past, past, past, past

Where?

Oh

Must

Must

Please

There

*A beautiful and massive black and white graffito
is revealed.*

On the wall between Gap and New Look
Huge and bold

In black and white

A rose

Perfect petals
Blooming out its circle centre

There isn't time but I stare

It must have took him hours

They'll never scrub that off. Never be the same again.

Oh let me climb in
Slip in between the spray and disappear cos I know he's in there

Now
time has gone

JOE appears with spray can in hand gasping for breath.

JOE: Pearl. What have you done?

He drops what he is holding and puts his hand out to her.

They're coming

PEARL puts her hand in his.

PEARL: Then we've got to run

They do.

SCENE 11

Joe's flat

Same morning

DEAN is standing behind his front door.

Holding a broom.

Sound of banging on door.

DEAN: I'll call the police. I'll call the police. I'll call the fucking
police. I fucking well will
Call the police.
What have I ever fucking done to…
he ain't here and I dunno where he is and if he was and if I did
I would say
FUCKING TAKE HIM ! He's a thieving little no good low life
fucking … he's nicked my fucking stash money little basterding
… he'd be better off with you…might find a use for him…fucking
gypping piking dirty tax avoiding fucking fucking fucking fucking
fucking fucking fucking fucking fucking fucking fucking FUCK
Turned me down didn't they the bolloxing banking bastards won't
give me the mortgage mortgage for me place in Bulg perfect it
was gonna be my place in the sun I worked hard all me fucking
life worth nothing went to work all me fucking life yes sir yes sir
yes sir paid the rent paid the mortgage paid me tax and National
fucking Insurance a couple of defaults didn't even know must have
got…difficult…didn't…wasn't keeping track…got a bit…would have
been worth it…all my fucking life……kept going to…those fuckers
in suits pushing bits of paper around credit credit credit…took all
me money for eighteen years of me life…keeping it all going……
On me own with him never had no one to help me
those fuckers on the telly how do they on those programmes get
the sea view?……fucking here I am stuck in this dump.
Be lucky now if I can keep it!

Tried to keep us on the straight and narrow
Always looked smart in his school uniform
Never went to fucking school!

Nicked from his own father

You can bang as much as you want
This door ain't coming…

Loud bang of door coming down.

Blackout.

…down.

SCENE 12

Under a flyover

Same morning.

Corridor of light.
Sound of cars above.

PEARL and JOE searching for the path to the site.

PEARL: I never been down there before

JOE: I ain't sure yer should be now Pearl

PEARL: Where's the path?

JOE: Are you sure she won't…

PEARL: I told yer

JOE: Yeah but…this…me!

PEARL: Lorraine always say. Since I were a little chavvy. 'If ye ever get into any troug. Whatever it be. Whatever. I will give help te thee.'

Still searching.

JOE: It's all concrete wall

PEARL: Here

JOE: Narrow init?

They move down it.

PEARL: Dunno how they get down here with prams and shopping

And into site.

JOE: It's freezing

Fuck what's?

PEARL: Scrap. Their work

JOE: Which one's hers?

PEARL: Be the trailer without a Virgin Mary in the window. Irish site

JOE: Oh

Stops. Whispers extra quiet.

Yer sure she won't grass us up?

PEARL: She keep her promise. She keep her word

Keep walking

He does.

JOE: Got window boxes

PEARL: Dunno how they keep flowers alive down here

Sound of a yappy dog barking.
JOE jumps.

JOE: Fuck

PEARL: (*To dog.*) Ssh.
Wiry little feck

Irish woman's voice comes out of darkness.

IRISH TRAVELLER: You's looking for someone?

PEARL: Lorraine and Alfie Lee

IRISH TRAVELLER: They was down at the end there. Moved on this morning

PEARL: Thanks

JOE: Fuck for that

Sound of engine coming close.

PEARL: Me Daddy's car!

JOE: Get behind here

They move into the darkness.

PEARL: Round here

JOE: Did he see us?

PEARL: Don't think

JOE: How d'yer?

PEARL: Know the sound

JOE: Get over

PEARL: Shit

I ain't a fucking whatsit fish

JOE: What?

PEARL: One of them things without no bones

JOE: Starfish

PEARL: Yeah… Shit……

JOE: It's your boobs…squeeze in and I'll pull

PEARL: Don't ye fucking…

JOE: Just your arm I'm pulllllllllling.

She falls through on top of him
into square of light.
They pause
tempted but.

Soft sound of horses.

PEARL: Got ta keep them grai quiet

JOE: What's the matter with 'em?

PEARL: They dunno who we are. Think we're burglars

JOE: It's alright. It's alright ssssssh

PEARL: Me and me mush is on the run

JOE: Her family is out there and if they find us they're gonna kill us

PEARL: They ain't gonna look in here

JOE: Unless you keep making that noise

PEARL: Stroke 'em

JOE: Can't reach over

PEARL: Round the front bit

JOE: Where?

PEARL: Ye scared of 'em?

JOE: No

PEARL: Ye are

JOE: Not

They gone quieter

PEARL: Cos ye threatening to touch 'em

JOE: Thought they wouldn't let 'em keep horses

PEARL: Not theirs. Stables for the posh kids in Notting Hill

JOE: Posh horses

PEARL: Don't smell like it

Touch me

She moves into him.

JOE: They're still out there

PEARL: They're not in here though

JOE: What if they find us?

PEARL: If they find us like this it'll be too late

JOE: Not to late ta churda me up

PEARL: Too late te marry Clive boy

JOE: Is that all I am te yer ? A way out from Clive boy?

PEARL: Yeah………come here

JOE: What's wrong with him anyway?

PEARL: He ain't ye

JOE: Why do yer like me?

PEARL: Ye ain't him

JOE: Go out to 'em
Before it's too late

PEARL: Make it too late

Thought ye was a man

Ye feel like a man

He pushes her hands away and holds them down.

She keeps kissing any parts of him she can reach.

JOE: When we do it…when we…it's got to be…somewhere…
where there's… blossoming

PEARL: Listen

Sound of engine.

They're going

Sound gets distant.

Where ye taking me then?

SCENE 13

Where the fence once was

That afternoon.

ANN is slightly deranged.

DEAN is on other side further up. She can't see him. He can hear her.

ANN: Is this where ye met him?
Story o shame Pearl
Betrayed ye own family
They out lookin fer ye now
An when they find ye I dunno what they……
I never should have said ye couldn't come with us
Come back and we'll straighten it out
Somehow
What people will say I don't
What else have we got?

DEAN walks towards her. He is dishevelled. Lost.
She jumps.
They stare at each other.

DEAN: If she got eyes like you I know why he done it

They stare some more.

I dunno where they've gone
I didn't know half of what he was about

ANN: Me husband told me. Ye didn't have a clue

DEAN: Thought they was gonna batter me. Didn't. Just looked.
Round the flat. Into me eyes

ANN: He still out there now.
He get her back

DEAN: What will they do to him?
If they find 'em. Will they bring 'em back here?
Will they?

ANN: I ain't accountable fer that.
Just want me daughter back in one…
She ain't gonna get no husband now.
Not after she been out a night… She'll have te stay with us
Help me like she always done.
She can start with the boxes.
Council sent us boxes
And bubble wrap!
Give us four days
Got the order this morning

Four days
Te jell

DEAN: To jell?

ANN: To LEAVE. To feckin LEAVE our home of seventeen year.
What if they can't find her?
How she find her way back to us?
What if we ain't here by then?
She never been away afore on her own

DEAN: She ain't on her own

ANN: She with your mochady son and the little bit of dosh he stole
from ye drugs stash That what ye fed him is it?
That what he's feeding her?

DEAN: He didn't take drugs

ANN: Ye all out o control

DEAN: Like you had control of your daughter

ANN: She had a good future
Marry a good man. Good family behind him. Love her proper
he would.
All cushti it were gonna be
Beautiful girl clean and …
Till ye mochady son followed her…found her
Whatever he did to her HERE

Pause.

What is it YE want HERE?
What is it YE be doing HERE?

DEAN: I were just walking
looking

ANN: HERE?
This is where they run from!

DEAN: What yer doing here then?

ANN: I LIVE HERE!

DEAN: Must be something about him. She fell in love with

ANN: She fell alright

DEAN: It were my fault. I told him I were going. That he had te get out. Find his own way

ANN: Joe. That's his name isn't it?

DEAN: He were searching for something. Found it in your daughter. I'm sorry.
What'll they do to him? Just send him back to me will yer. I'll deal with him. Just send him back te me

ANN: We knows where ye are.
Where we be
Who knows?
Even the rats here is moving on
See 'em scurrying over the mounds o rubble and under the fences every night.
Might have te go in an house
Or flat
Kelly and Nathan boy goin to his people
Alice she…

DEAN: Never seen a grown man a big man like yer husband cry like that.

ANN: Ye not shedding a tear fer yer son?

DEAN: I ain't cried for years

ANN: She ain't even got a change o clothes
Pearl!
Where she gonna sleep?
ye feckin son has…
When ye see yer son Joe buried up to ears in this concrete them trucks be carrying with no cory cos they cut it off ye's might remember how te cry

DEAN: Cory?

ANN: Penis

SCENE 14

A wood

Same afternoon.

JOE and PEARL are loosely wrapped up in an old blanket.
Relaxed.
They are surrounded by a pattern made of wild flowers.

PEARL: Do it again

JOE: Were it beautiful Pearl?

PEARL: It were

JOE: The most beautiful thing?

PEARL: The most beautiful

JOE: (*Whispers.*) Give me me story then. The last story left

PEARL: Ye got te do it again Joe. Make sure that weren't
beginner's bok – luck

She wraps herself around him.

JOE: I gotta eat Pearl

He kisses her and slowly tries to get away but she won't let go.

PEARL: Ain't ye got no more peanuts left?

JOE: I need more than peanuts to keep up with yer

She pulls him closer he succumbs for a bit but…

I'm gonna faint Pearl

PEARL: Lightweight

JOE: I ain't eaten in a day

PEARL: I haven't neither

JOE: We gotta go to that village and get some food

PEARL: Stay here. We'll go tomorrow

JOE: I'll be dead by tomorrow

He sits up.

It's broken now? The song he give to you?

PEARL: It's broken now

He gets up and puts his jeans on.

Ye can't. Go. What if someone comes?

JOE: Better come with me then

PEARL: Pass us me toggs then

He does. She gets dressed under the blanket.

The last story. Me rarest one. If it be told to someone who
ain't ready
Is a dangerous thing
Is so dazzling
could blind ye like the suns rays bleedin into ye eyes.
But if ye be ready
not only will it bind the one ye love tight to ye forever and ever
It will show ye the way in times of troug
A glistening path in the darkest night

JOE: I'm ready now. Don't yer think?

He goes to kiss her.

PEARL: I forgot it Joe

JOE: Then I'm gonna make you remember it

She runs up onto low branch of a tree.

*He circles her
and snarls.*

PEARL: Can't ye climb a tree Joe?

He grabs her leg to pull her down.

JOE: Be careful Pearl or I might do something really brave

She kicks him off.

PEARL: How ye gonna do that from there?

*As he reaches her branch
she jumps down.*

It starts raining. A deluge.

*The whole wood starts to rock and vibrate with sudden LOUD sound of a
festival starting up.
Rubicks playing 'Red Rock'.*

*They freeze in amazement.
Then look up, at each other and then out towards the festival field that
the sound is coming from.*

What is it?

JOE: Looks like a festival Pearl.
A festival!

*PEARL climbs up the tree again. Fast. Frightened. Intrigued. Gets close to
him then pulls herself up onto tiptoes to look.*

PEARL: Them people!

JOE: I didn't know!
Weren't what I meant…
Wouldn't have been like this when your Granny lived here?

PEARL: Peace and quiet then

JOE: They're just havin' fun

PEARL: Dicken the rom and raklis togs kai!

JOE: Their havin' their holidays

PEARL: Spend whole lives slave to a house and then soon as
they get the chance
Go in a tent.
From B&Q

JOE: Think they'd do it all the time if they could

PEARL: Why don't they then? Why don't they do it?

PEARL and JOE: Jobs

PEARL: Too much education
'ocrites

Hate us fer being free
Finish our way o life

JOE: I ain't got no education

PEARL: Na, ye got me

PEARL jumps down.

JOE: Come on then

He takes her hand, she pulls away.

PEARL: I ain't goin in there with them people

JOE: You might like it

PEARL: How am I gonna like it?

JOE: Don't like it then

He moves to go.

PEARL: Ye ain't coming back are ye? Had ye taste o Gypsy flesh
and off te them hippie raklis all covered in mud and nothing else

JOE: I'll come back as quick as.
With something 'll keep us going through all the night

PEARL: You'll never stop?

JOE: Only for food
What shall I get yer?

PEARL: What 'ave they got?

JOE: Come with me an see

PEARL: I ain't going in that bit where they all squished up

JOE: Yer don't have to. Just to the food stalls till we find
something yer fancy

PEARL: I know what I

JOE: Yer won't if I lose me strength

PEARL: There's so many of 'em…

She holds back.

He starts to walk away.

JOE: Didn't think you'd be scared Pearl

PEARL: I might not be here when ye come back

JOE: I better take yer with me then

He picks her up.
She thumps him and jumps down.

PEARL: I ain't lost the use of me legs. Ye weren't that good

She picks up a rose then puts it behind her ear.

Dance with me Joe. Dance with me

He dances over to her – ravey sort of dancing.

I ain't dancing like that!

JOE: It's free Pearl. We're free!

PEARL: It ain't free. It's divvy

JOE: Come on

PEARL: Do it proper like

Might help me remember

JOE: Alright

He stops and formally puts out his hand to her.

May I have this dance?

She accepts. Awkward at first. He doesn't know the steps. She leads him.
It gets wilder and wilder till they don't know who is leading who and
somehow end up back up the tree.
Music stops.

PEARL: Come on then

Prove ye ready

Pushes him up against the trunk.

Make it all worth it
Make it worth it

Make it worth

She pulls his t shirt off.
He manoeuvres her around and pushes her up against trunk
drops to his knees
kisses her feet
then
kisses and bites his way up her body.
Lights fade as he begins to lift her t shirt.

SCENE 15

The trailer

Same afternoon.

ANN is manically cleaning the Waterford glassware.

GRANNY LOVERIDGE comes in with piles of newspaper and bubble wrap out of which she pulls a bottle of whiskey.

ANN: Nathan boy's sitting outside their flat

GRANNY: What fer? He ain't coming back with her

GRANNY takes two glasses from the Waterford shelf.

ANN: Should ha beaten him off afore

GRANNY: Wouldn't done no good

ANN: I'll Hoover up you get on with ye reading and writing.
That's what I used te tell her
Made her think different

GRANNY: Don't make the gorgers think none

ANN: Clive boy's thrashed his trailer. News travels fast if nix else do

GRANNY pours glasses half full of whiskey.
They drink.
ANN starts polishing figurine.

Me Daddy give ye this

GRANNY: Second week we was married. Sold his best grai fer it
Bleedin' bleeder. Wherever he be now

ANN: She's coming back

GRANNY: She ain't coming back

ANN: She coming back!

GRANNY: Te what?

ANN: What's he gonna feed her? Them drugs?. He'll have her
prostituting…turn her into some hedge mumper…

GRANNY: Put that down. Ye cleaned it thrice already.

She does but takes another.

ANN: Should ha given her a phone when she wanted one.
She can't even send me a little note if she wanted te
bastards stopped the feckin post

GRANNY: She done best thing she could.
Not sitting stuck years going past with the traffic

GRANNY pulls a cardboard box out from under their window seat.

ANN: That's not what ye said when me daddy go

GRANNY: We been alright

ANN: Leavin Pearl newborn

GRANNY: Stuck still same view day after day.
Nix to look forward to no grai to tend
he couldn't help it

ANNY: That's not what others say

GRANNY: I know what they say
And so does he.
He have to live with their judgement like we have to live with
his loss
Ye can't stop a soul from following their heart
An I didn't mind
After he had all his teeth ta'en out
An me boobs gone saggy
We had our time

ANN: If he here Pearl wouldn't ha'

GRANNY: Ye the one that wanted a pretty life

ANN: We couldn't have gone on like!

GRANNY: No
There weren't no going on
Not with all the 'strictions

ANN: Moved on every two day

GRANNY: If she here or no
Getting married or no
Might as well put that in a box
We still getting
Shifted

GRANNY takes figurine from ANN.

It's finished Ann. It's over

ANN takes figurine back.

GRANNY: This life is heaven. Hell is what we make it

ANN: I ain't livin on that feckin playground!

GRANNY: Take our chances

ANN: They've took all our chances

GRANNY: Ye forget yeself?

Living here all these years
With ye comforts an ye washing machine

ANN: I done it fer ye
When this site come up permanent.
Couldn't ha gone on moving frem one long tail infested mumpley
hole te the next.
Weren't allowed te stop nowhere decent no more.
Ye gen dinlow forget what it were like?

I were bory! With Pearl

ANN smashes figurine.

GRANNY: And Pearl took her chance soon as she saw it

On the move
like a bleedin Gypsy

SCENE 16

The wood

Next day.

PEARL is hanging out her washing on a branch by the tent.
She is wrapped in the blanket. Her hair is wet.
JOE enters excitedly with hamburgers and beers and tampax.
PEARL hears him but turns her back to him.

JOE: They're all talking about you Pearl.
In the festival field
Pearl?
I got you what yer…

Holds out some tampax. She snatches them.

And some food

He offers her a hamburger while he eats his.

PEARL: I ain't eating that

She goes behind tent with a bottle of water.

JOE: You ate eaten nothing but bananas

PEARL: I'll go te the bakers tomorrow. In the village.
If ye'll give me back the money I earnt

JOE: I spent it Pearl

PEARL: It weren't yours te spend

JOE: It were only a few quid

PEARL: It were my few quid. We ain't married

JOE: Didn't think it were Romanies who were funny about beef

PEARL: Ain't got nothing te do with beef

JOE: What then? I looked at the stall and everything it was clean

PEARL: Them festival people. Might have put drugs in.
Ye shouldn't eat it

JOE: They ain't gonna give away free drugs with the burgers.
Wouldn't be none left.
(*Laughs.*) Burger dealers

He eats.

Can't live on fresh air

PEARL: Can't live without it

She comes out and takes the beer.

Ye left me in the water

JOE: I got what you needed

PEARL: I didn't ask ye to

JOE: I didn't mind

PEARL: It ain't men's business

JOE: I'm a sissy gorger

PEARL: It weren't meant to be now…it were…

JOE: You liked it in the water though. Didn't you
Pearl?

PEARL: Thou knowest I did

JOE: In the stream I found for yer

Them fishes didn't bite yer did they?

PEARL: No

JOE: Told yer. Fish kisses. Tiny fish kisses all over

He kisses her neck. Her shoulders. She stops him going any further.

What did you say to that girl that come to yer?

They're all buzzin about you. Askin' each other.
'Are you gonna go and see that Gypsy, she's a real Romany you
know, won't be any left soon…in a few years' time…'

'Tell yer things no one else could know. Just by looking at
your palm'

Another girl say she always wanted to meet a real one. She's got an
old caravan in her garden painted all red and gold

PEARL: It's called a vardo

JOE: Cost a bomb. Saw some at Appleby Fair
We could get one of them
An old vardo
One day
There's gonna be lots more tenners Pearl
And double that. For couples
Been drumming up business Pearl

PEARL: Ye said ye was coming back fer me.
I waited. In the water

JOE: I knew you'd find yer way.
Got busy
Got a list

Pulls one out.

With appointments
If yer did 15 singles and five couples a day that that's…

PEARL: That's 250 quid a day
And what are ye gonna do?

JOE: I'll be your business manager Pearl

PEARL: Is that what ye call it?

JOE: I found you a stream Pearl

You said you wanted to wash

PEARL: What if a man had come?

JOE: What?

PEARL: Me on me own no clothes on in the stream. If a man
had come. No one there to protect me

JOE: The fish were there

PEARL: What if they did?

JOE: I wanted to get yer what yer needed

PEARL: You didn't come back though

JOE: Pearl I knew you'd be alright. Seized the moment.
Thought you'd be pleased. 'Bout the business

PEARL just looks at him.

It were your idea to do it

PEARL: I know it were mine

JOE: Mesmerising 'em with yer original gypsy in the woods thing
'Tell ye fortune fer a little ten'

PEARL: Ye story come back to me Joe. In the water. After ye left
me. It were swimming with ye fishes. Its colours are strong Joe.
Dazzling through the water. Hard te catch. So rare. Ye weren't there
te give it to. Slipped through me fingers.

JOE: I were getting you what I yer needed!
You had blood all over your jeans
Trying te hide it with your jacket
An you wouldn't let me

PEARL: I couldn't…!

JOE: But you could in the water.
It were like a cool bath weren't it?

PEARL: I told ye I ain't never been in a bath before

JOE: Better than any shower

A few more o them fortunes and we'll get a beautiful old vardo.
We'll do all the festivals

PEARL: An we'll follow the seasons across the country in it
drawn by a unicorn?

JOE: They'll be coming soon. For an appointment

PEARL: I ain't ready fer 'an appointment'

JOE: What did she say to yer Pearl?
The girl that come to yer in the tent this morning?

Why won't yer tell me?
Were it secrets?
Pearl?
Well what did she say to you then?

PEARL: She say, 'Wow this tent is awesome where can I get one?'

JOE: Did yer tell her pull a bit of tarpaulin off the side the road?

PEARL: I say, 'Give me ye palm dearie' then
'Oh dordy
Ye've had a difficult time haven't ye dear
Life's been hard on ye hasn't it?'
And she give me
her bracelet to read
'But ye gonna have a long life
And
Oh
What's this?
Oh yes
And ye do deserve it don't ye dear
A beautiful house and what a garden and
There be
Oh
There is someone ye've to BEWARE of
DANGER
Who is it?
Can't quite see
Getting a bit hazy
If ye could just see ye way te give me a little more I might be
able te see clearly dear'
And she says she can give me a fiver but don't have no change and
I say that's alright dear and I take the tenner what's in her hand
and she say, 'Thank you'

JOE: I didn't know yer could do that

PEARL: Neither did I Joe
'Now,' I say, 'Does ye know a woman with a name beginning with
A, B, C or D?'
And she look even blanker than before in her eyes so I say 'Is it
D E F or G is it?

75

I think it might be an H?'
Her eyes light up a bit
So I says 'H yes BEWARE a woman whose name begins with H'

And she say, 'I knew
I knew I couldn't trust her'

And then it took me over. Like it were doing it on its own

'But it don't matter dear, cos that special someone, ye haven't met
him yet but if ye keep ye eyes open for a lovely man he's wearing
them brown Wellington things, black jeans with a rip over the right
thigh, a green t shirt an there's a thin bit of cotton or something
round his neck and he's got a speck of brown in his blue eyes.
His hair is blond he's pushing it back with his hand.
He will love ye and lead ye onto the right path.
And that dear
is that – fer now
I tired out'

She yawns theatrically.

'I ain't got no more te give ye
Not even a bit o gold fer comfort
Cos ye know ye should never take gold from a Gypsy
But a Gypsy can take gold from ye and ye know it will bring ye
luck like ye never had and most important of all dear it will bring
ye protection'
And that were when she takes off this amulet from her bracelet and
place it down in front of me and say, 'Thank you very much'

JOE: It's true what they say then, beware of them Gypsies they'll put
a spell on yer and take all yer gold

PEARL: It were only a few quid

JOE: An an amulet her old Mum give her

PEARL: It weren't!
Shouldn't have been taken in

JOE: Like me you mean

PEARL: Ye got the true Romany

76

JOE: Did I?
Did yer Granny teach yer to lie like that?

PEARL: How do ye know it were lies?

JOE: Weren't it?

PEARL: I dunno.
It just come to me

They both look out.

JOE: They're coming Pearl.
Get ready.
Sit in the tent

PEARL: I'm wearing the feckin' tent Joe

JOE: Then put yer fucking clothes on

PEARL: They're wet

He runs to them. The clothes on the line. Feels them as he pulls them off the line and thrusts them at her.

JOE: Nearly dry.
That girl said something 'bout finding her fella with the speck in his eye.
Loads of 'em wanna see yer

PEARL: No!

JOE: Get in the tent!
The festival's over tonight. Gotta make the most of it

PEARL: I didn't stop telling that girl's fortune cos I were tired.
I stopped cos of what I saw!
An again in the water
It weren't ye's story I saw in the water. It were mine.
Mixing up with yer red fishes. Turned te flame. All I could see were yog. Couldn't look no more. Felt the flames on me face

JOE: What else we gonna do?

PEARL: I don't wanna get me eyes burnt

JOE: Get in the tent

He grabs her
and pushes her backwards towards tent.

She frees herself.

PEARL: No!
I don't want te!

She rips down the tarpaulin.
He lunges at her.

JOE: What the fuck do you want?

SCENE 17

The trailer

Same day.

Olympic flags flying high in the sky.

ANN is wrapping up the china and glass in newspaper and packing it
away in boxes.

GRANNY is half watching her half looking out of window.

GRANNY: A stain on the sky

She leaves.

Sound of bulldozers.

GRANNY is climbing up onto roof of trailer.

ANN: What the feck?

GRANNY: Bulldozers. Like a waiting swarm o…

ANN runs outside.

ANN: Couldn't even wait fer us te…
They ain't spose te be here fer another two day

GRANNY: Who they waiting fer that's what I wanna know.
The feckin bailiffs.

ANN runs back inside. Starts throwing things out of boxes.

GRANNY half climbs half jumps of roof and into trailer.

Ye won't find it in there.

ANN: Where ye hid it?

GRANNY pulls her jumper up to reveal the story belt around her waist.

GRANNY: Granny Coulson give this me and only one person
allowed te look in it

ANN: An' she ain't here

GRANNY: No. She gone on

ANN: That story might tell us where

GRANNY: That story is fer Pearl

ANN: She ain't never gonna get it now is she?

GRANNY: Can ye see the future?

ANN: Nay but ye can…
ye could…
Till……

GRANNY: *It* stopped me Ann.
The power.
Just after Pearl were born. After we stopped moving.
It stopped me
seeing

Pause.

ANN: Sometimes we'd do 600 hundred doors a day

GRANNY: Got loaded these pockets on a good day

ANN: When ye thought they'd be biting and say, 'Shall I have
a look at ye palm dearie?'

And if she say, 'Yes,' and offer her pretty palm

GRANNY: Weren't always pretty

ANN: No
But her face were when she listen to what ye saw. You never said
the same thing twice not never to 'em as ye looked on the lines in
their palms and the shape o their fingers and tell 'em what they
wanted te know

GRANNY: And it weren't always good

ANN: But it were always true
You would never say if it were or no but I knew it were cos
'It marvellous what she can see in one's hand'

GRANNY: Gorger believe what they want te

ANN: And whenever we came back te those parts they'd ask fer
ye or say, 'You're Gypsy Betsy aren't ye?' and they'd say, 'Come in,
come in,' cos they wanted to hear what was going te happen te them
and they'd listen so close like and their eyes would look so light and
like new lives inside 'em was starting and I loved it I loved every
second o that.
And when I had Pearl inside me body she always give a little twist
like she were turning te hear it too.
Hearing them fortune stories always somehow give us…

Then
the stories became the same
started to tell 'em the same things
Over and over
Whoever it were

GRANNY: Couldn't see no different then
Couldn't see…

ANN: Every time it were same over and over
like our lives

And then ye stopped

GRANNY: It stopped me Ann. It stopped me

Pause.

ANN: I saw……
Last night.
That belt
Filling up me dreams
with
dead stories

GRANNY: Stories can't die. Tuti gins that

ANN: Then dick in te see kai

GRANNY: Ain't fer me te dick in adni

Fer us te let new ones be born

ANN: Find me daughter

GRANNY: She made her choice!

ANN: If she ever wanna see us agin……

GRANNY: If Pearl want te find us she find a way te it

ANN: How she gonna find a way when we can't?

Ye've gotta look

If not in there (*Gestures to belt.*) then wherever it were that gave ye the view. Like ye had. Before.
Like ye can. Tell her we gotta shift That it's starting. Now. Tell Her!

Or ye forget yeself too?

SCENE 18

The wood

Same day.

PEARL is crouched down, in front of a dead rabbit.

JOE is watching. In disbelief.

JOE: You've killed it

PEARL: Right between the eyes. First time

She picks it up.

He moves away.

Give me ye knife

JOE: What for? It's dead

PEARL: Give me the knife

He does. With trepidation.

She snatches it, looks at him with disdain, then places her rabbit down on a bed of leaves and starts skinning it, intently.

Get wood. And a bit fer a skewer. We'll put this on it. Up at the top

JOE: What the fuck for Pearl?

PEARL: What the feck do yer think? To cook this on.
Ye couldn't fucking catch it.
Or kill it
Or skin it
Maybe ye can GET THE WOOD TO COOK IT on

Goes back to the skinning.

JOE: How do'yer expect me to know how to kill a fucking rabbit.
I ain't cruel to animals.
I ain't never practised

PEARL: Neither have I

Quietly:

Must be in me blood

JOE: You don't know how to skin it though do yer?

PEARL: See – comes off just like a jacket and strides. First the arms…

JOE: It ain't coming off

PEARL: It will

JOE: (*Disgusted.*) Yer just making a mess!

PEARL: Get the wood

JOE: Pearl – all the flesh is coming off with it

PEARL: (*To herself.*) Scrape it off

JOE: Pearl…it's…bury it. Let's bury it.
We'll go back to the village and I'll get us some sandwiches

PEARL: I didn't come all the way here to eat feckin sandwiches!
I could make sandwiches on the feckin site in Hackney! I wanna eat
this. Wild chushi here. What I caught

Right between the eyes

Blood spurts out of the rabbit.

JOE: (*Horrified.*) Pearl! What yer…?

PEARL: Rabbit heart. Good fer ye

JOE: It's all on yer blanket!

PEARL: Get the wood

JOE: Stop it Pearl. Stop. We're gonna bury it

PEARL: We gonna eat it

He tries to take it from her. She resists.
Both get blood-soaked.
He holds her wrist tight till she drops the heart.
He tries to cover it up with leaves.
She kicks him in the side.
He falls sideways. Gets up
and grabs her shoulders.
He doesn't know what to do with her – or himself.

GET THE WOOD

JOE: I dunno what fucking wood to get!

PEARL: Kindling

JOE: I dunno what it looks like!

PEARL: Neither do I!

She punches him in the face.

He stands there.
She punches him again.
He stands there.
Again.
He wobbles back then comes forward and grabs her between the legs.
She stands there. On tiptoes.
A moment.
Then:

Give me ye lighter

JOE: I've lost it

PEARL: It's in ye's pocket. I saw ye put it there

She grabs the wrist of his hand that is holding her but can't pull it free.

They are frozen.

JOE: Why do yer want it?

PEARL: So when *I'VE* collected the wood *I* can light the fire like
I do everything
Cos ye ain't got no capabilities
No
not even one
not even *that*

After I left me whole past and future fer ye
ye
Brimson
Gorger
Wannabe

Let me go and give me that lighter
Afore I put a curse on ye

JOE: I think yer already done that Pearl.
why would I ever ave come here
With you
Otherwise?

If yer want my lighter – yer better say please

PEARL:

JOE: Say it

PEARL:

JOE: OK

He lets her go.

Come and get it

*She goes to him and to put her hand in his pocket but he grabs her wrist
and twists her arm behind her back.*

Say please

He pushes her down to her knees.

Cos yer gonna need it.
Pearl.

In a minute I'll be gone
and tonight
the festival will be gone
an you'll be here
alone with your dead rabbit
an then what yer gonna do?
No one te do yer weird fortune shit on
No one te help yer wash
No one te make yer feel like a woman

Say it

She twists around suddenly and bites his leg viciously.

He pulls her off by the neck and holds her down there.

The true Romany
No wonder you didn't wanna marry Clive boy
Yer knew
Soon as he saw what was inside yer he'd leave yer at the side
of the road
Like the dirty little bitch that ye are

He lets her go.
She doesn't move.

He collects bits of wood
randomly and throws them in a heap by the rabbit.

There's yer wood.
And here's yer bone little dog little jukel should I say

Drops the lighter
and stamps it into the rabbit.

fetch

He goes to walk off.

She darts towards and grabs the knife from the earth holds it in her teeth as
she runs at him and pulls his legs from under him pushes him onto his front
and kneels on his arms with all her might. She grips the knife in her hands
and points it towards his heart – rips away a bit of his t-shirt.

PEARL: It would be so easy
So easy
Bit by bit
little pieces

Waits.

But I ain't gonna
Na
Don't like the taste of ye

Never did

She gets up but holds the knife still pointing it at him.

That's why I lied te ye about the story
I never had it
Weren't never mine te give ye

They stare at each other for a long time.
Then
he leaves.

She rearranges wood.
Pulls lighter from rabbit.
Tries to make lighter work.
Over and over.
Tries rubbing sticks together.
Nothing.
She crumples
in front of the wood.

SCENE 19

The wood

That night.
PEARL is still huddled by the wood.
The fire ignites itself and shoots into huge flames which
GRANNY appears through.

GRANNY: I were born on a beach
Me birth certificate scratched into a rock

I ain't goin in no
house
No flat
Put us in a box afore
Them walls
Nothing te step out te
None of me people round me
Don't put ye together
Neighbours find out
Paint on the doors
Nasty packets through the letterbox
Torture ye mind it would

An' I ain't goin back on the Drom
Not now Pearl
Like it is
Too old
It's finished Pearl
Days of horse-drawn are gone
I'm staying here with me china

Pulls photo out of her apron.

I found a photograph o your granddaddy I'd forgotten.
He were standin next te the Queen
I were there that day. At the pageant. Snapped it meself

He see a horse he liked happened te be standing next te the
Queen so he jumped over the fence so he get a picture with the
'andsome grai! Not bothered 'bout the Queen

The Council want us gone.
Whole world wants us gone.
Time fer their Games
Bulldozers are here. Bailiffs on the way
Think they can sneak up on us early

Yesterday's dead, tomorrow's yet te come, today's what we live fer!

An today 'll be me last one Pearl.
Me dearest little Pearl.
I'll see ye in the next world
If there be one

Remember yeself.
What ye are

GRANNY steps back into the flames and disappears.

PEARL: AND WHAT AM I THEN?

Come back!!!!!

Noooooooooooooo

Ye can't
Ye can't
YE CAN'T

I can't
Do
It
without
Ye

I thought I could
but I can't

That's why I come out here
To find out what's in me blood

What am I spose te de?
With ye blood in me veins
In me HEART?

Ye told me te follow it
me heart
An I did

Cos ye wouldn't let me
Come with ye

wanted me te live in a cage

Safe
Safe!

Ye hated it too didn't ye?
Ye last years
Since I were born
When ye stopped

Moving
Feeling
Seeing
Being

Least before
ye went travelling
an' had grai

If it is the end fer ye
then
WHAT ABOUT ME?!

Moves right up to flames.

Give me me story!
It were left te me
Ye said I could have it when I were ready
Well

I'm ready now!
Give it me!

Snap to black.

SCENE 20

The wood

Bit before dawn that night.

PEARL is sitting by the wood.

*JOE enters cautiously
a little way in with a bottle of water.
She hears him, looks up but not at him.*

JOE: The festival's gone Pearl.
It's gone now

I went to the stream. Followed the fish right into the dark water.
Were black and still like death but I kept swimming through
till the fish brought me up the other side
blue
Filled this up

thought you might want to…

Moves a little closer to her.

I didn't mean any of it
Pearl
What I said
What I did
Pearl
I'm glad I got beat up so many times in me life
Deserved it fer what I done to thee
I'd…

PEARL: Give me me jacket

He gets it and very gently puts it around her shoulders, kneeling behind her.

I never had the power Joe.
till ye came
got a flash
just afore

of everything I ever wanted

then
there ye were
at the fence
like an animal
wounded

all me dreams in thee

JOE: Its gonna be alright Pearl. Everything you said about me were true I know it but I'm gonna think of something I dunno how I'm gonna do I dunno what I'm gonna if it kills me Pearl I'm gonna make it alright make it up

PEARL: Touch me

*She reaches up and puts her arms around his neck, without turning.
He is still behind her.*

JOE: You want me to?

He ever so gently turns her to face him.

PEARL: I love it Joe.

I love ye.
Always have
Always will

Nothin can be done 'bout that

JOE: Pearl

PEARL: Let's close our yox Joe

She delicately sweeps her fingers over his eyes. Then closes her own.

Close 'em and keep 'em closed

They kiss like nothing else exists.
Lights fade.
When they come up again.
She is gone.

JOE wakes up.
Jumps to his feet.

JOE: Pearl?

Picks up the blanket.

Looks around him.

Can feel *it*

(*Quietly.*) They've taken her

back

Pours some water over his head and drinks from bottle.
Pulls his clothes on.

I'm coming Pearl

Runs off.

I'm coming

SCENE 21

The site that was

It is daylight.
Low sound of bulldozers.
All that is left is GRANNY's burnt out trailer. Broken glass and rubble.
PEARL is crouching in the doorway of the trailer
with the story belt.
She turns it upside down.
Empty.

PEARL: All the plots was empty
They'd pulled off 'em all
Trailers hitched to the cars
ready te
jell
I could see in te down here from up there
That hilly bit with the dead tree
Just me Granny's old trailer left
all her china
still there
displayed
in the window
Me Mum an' Alice and Kelly went in closed the curtains
The lines on me Mum's face
Dripping with sorrow
Kelly had to hold her up
small steps they took
te
join me dad
Nathan boy
The Smiths
The Lees
The Connors
Old Prices
Biltons
An them Rileys

Noah boy holding on te little Davy boy
all the chavvies went still
everyone

stood round
in a circle
Faces full o endings
Me dad covered Granny's trailer with petrol
came back
me mum lit the flame
on his old lighter
They all moved back together
she threw it in
like a rocket it sounded
when it blew
Glass smashing with the china
flames jumping straight up
takin me Granny and her stuff
free and clean into the air
by the time fire engines got in burnt out
just this left
hot shell

If I'd gone down would ha made it worse
What would I say to 'em?
Now

Bailiffs had bin in the morn
Put their enforcement orders on
And now
gavvers waiting
Escort 'em out
Kept their heads up they did
Me people
Didn't look down
Nor
Never heard 'em so quiet
Just the gravel neath the feet
Got in the trailers and cars
drove out

Gavvers' cars in front with silent sirens
just the blue whizzing round
And behind
an' at the sides

gavvers' grai too
Blinkers on
Like they didn't wanna see the history inside
All gone
Wished they'd thrown 'em off
Wish them grai had thrown 'em gavvers off their backs and
galloped out inte the traffic
Galloped out all across London

JOE appears.

JOE: If they had I'd go out and catch yer one Pearl.
The most beautiful white grai

PEARL: An we'd ride off down Hackney High Road?

I can't go to 'em
me poor family
Even if I knew where they was
Shame I bought on 'em
they'd hide me in the trailer be the scivvy rackli all me life

JOE: Come out with me
Can't stay here
It's dangerous if yer people catch yer if the police…

PEARL: Am I trespassing?

JOE: Come out onto the street Pearl

She shows him the story belt.

Is that?

She turns it upside down.

DEAN enters.

DEAN: I thought it was you
I thought it was
Saw you back there on the street
Joe

Grabs him to him and bursts into tears.

Stupid little
You can't stay here. Shouldn't be here

Come back with me. Both of you

JOE: What happened to Bulg?

DEAN: Didn't work out. But something will.
Being repossessed but…

JOE: You're homeless too

DEAN: Not yet I ain't. Got a couple of weeks…
Let's get out of here
Come on

JOE: Pearl?

He starts to move towards her. She stops him.

I ain't leaving you here

PEARL: I ain't ready.
In a bit

JOE: I'm waiting outside then. Just out there

PEARL: In a bit

He leaves with DEAN.

She picks up the story belt and winds it round her wrist and arm.

Or

Maybe
I'll take me chances

cos
stories never die
They just go back into the ground
with all the other stories that have ever been lost

waiting

just

waiting

She moves her head towards the sky and looks into the sun.

The End.

Glossary
of
Romany words

Adni Here

Atchin Tan Stopping place

Bok Luck

Bory Pregnant

Brimson Bullshitter

Chavvy Child

Chored Stolen

Chushi Rabbit

Cory Penis

Cushti Good

Del Give

Dick Look

Dinlow Fool

Divvy Silly

Drom Road

Duckering Fortune telling

Gavvers Police

Gorger Non gypsies

Grai Horse (*pronounced 'Gry', as in 'cry'*)

Hawking Selling

Hedge mumper Tramp

Hokie Lie

Hotchiwitchi Hedgehog

Jell Go

Jukel Dog

Kai There

Mandi Me

Mochady Unclean

Mumpley Inferior form of Gypsy

Mush Friend, man

Nix Nothing

Parnie Water

Patron Sign

Rai Gentleman

Rakli Woman or girl

Rokker Speak

Rom Man

Shraddhā (*Pronounced 'Shrad-AH', with the stress on the second syllable. A Sanskrit word, not Romany. But the Romany language comes from Sanskrit.*) It means Faith – that which is placed in the heart. You are what's in your heart

Starry Prison

Strides Trousers (*slang word*)

Togs Clothes

Troug Trouble

Tutti Jins Thou Knowest

Yog Fire

Yox Eyes

Vardo Traditional Caravan